angel falls

isbn: 978-0-578-29681-4

angel falls

a collection of poetry
by cheyanne leonardo

Cardinal Grosbeak.

for leann daniel
in her loving memory

july 15, 1997 - october 9, 2021

"wholeheartedly, like a child, i believe in magic."

- *a letter from leann*, may 14, 2021

and for you - *always*
the master of light -
the luminous magician
and the love of my life

dear reader,

this collection of poetry is both a love letter and a eulogy: it holds many moments of gratitude for our earthly life and endeavors to look beyond it through thoughtful exploration and unfettered imagination. the context for it all is the book's title – *angel falls* – which is a place as well as a concept.

first of all, *angel falls* is a real place. it is the ghost of a split-stream waterfall in my hometown's backyard, the big south fork, that was blasted with dynamite in 1954 to better accommodate boating and fishing. now it's a river rapid that causes confusion for hikers (expecting to arrive at the non-existent, hallowed falls) and extreme danger for kayakers and canoers (paddling downstream and navigating the perilous rock formation left behind).

but *angel falls* becomes a concept as soon as we shift our focus on the word "falls" from noun to verb. an angel falling. a fallen angel. what does such an image conjure, in this particular place and time? at least, within these pages, it is a celebration of the divine beauty we can perceive in this world and an attempt to accept that so many of our deepest questions will remain unanswered until we leave it. in the meantime, we love each other. and we try to understand our purpose here together.

ultimately, place and concept work together here. i love my home for its natural wonder, warmth, and curiosity. and i adore the people who make it such a marvelous, mystifying, and mystical place. i want this book to feel like it belongs both the scott county, tennessee, and to every last star in the sky. to me, both are equally infinite in their importance and complexity.

if our eyes are truly open, our only option is to look around, gaze into the depths, and learn all that we can from what is shown (and not shown) to us. there is love and life in every breathing corner, even when it appears shrouded in a cloud of loss and death.

writing this book gave me comfort in times of sadness and direction in many, many moments of joy. i hope these words, cascading from my heart, will pour into yours and offer you a little something, too.

love always,
cheyanne

the poet's eye, in a fine frenzy rolling,
doth glance from heaven to earth, from earth to heaven;
and as imagination bodies forth
the forms of things unknown, the poet's pen
turns them to shapes, and gives to airy nothing
a local habitation and a name.

-theseus, *a midsummer night's dream* by william shakespeare

i hide myself within my flower,
that wearing on your breast,
you, unsuspecting, wear me too —
and angels know the rest.

i hide myself within my flower,
that, fading from your vase,
you, unsuspecting, feel for me
almost a loneliness.

-emily dickinson

table of contents

window

there is no window here
on this first night
i open something lost
shut between skin and salt
how streams of sleep appeared
like death
bleeding out
and we did not see the dawn
the dark
the echo
the star
it was always only half a home
in this house
breath
world
but then i walked with you and said
come
come
come

cheyanne leonardo

angela

and isn't it easy to see
why she would be loved, wild
as wind moves through new leaves:
it's how she keeps kindness
right at her fingertips, grasps it
the way we would hold roses;
and every morning braids curiosity
into her hair, breathes
gentle bravery into the air.
it's how she opens her heart so wide
to new places, pulls back closed lips,
leaves smiles on faces. how she honors herself
as part of all the world, knows
borders between
are permeable,
knows that what she releases into the stream
evaporates,
only to fall again, wash over like rain.
it's everything her soul pours out
cup by cup — love
empties easily, but then —
forever fills back up.

glass swan

a little glass swan sits atop an old
cigar box that holds all my postcards. tall as
a thumbprint with wings forever spread above
her umbrella-handle neck, she leans forward,
ready to erupt from the river vltava in flight.

snowy white and marble smooth, she makes her home
here in my bedroom. but she comes from somewhere
far away. from prague. i swaddled her carefully in
layers of bubble wrap and newspaper, tucked her
into the pocket of my backpack, and carried her as
we flew together over continents and oceans. she is
not expensive or particularly valuable. but she is
a souvenir, in the french sense. a memory. a reminder.
i bought her from a golden-skinned man in a tour-
ist shop in the bitter cold of january so i would
remember what i had seen.

i walked over the charles bridge and looked out
over periwinkle water. the bright sun commanded
the gentle current of the vltava to glimmer and
glisten, and the water obeyed; although the sun's
power did little to warm the freezing air that pushed
pins and needles into my skin, despite my many layers
of clothing. i watched the swans glide along the tide.

the day before, i had taken a walking tour of the
city. i learned that a princess who once lived in
the castle overlooking the river had such an affinity
for the swans that she bestowed names upon each and
every one of them. she could tell them apart by the
way they arched their necks and flapped their wings.

i examined the swans swimming in the
water below. i tried to differentiate one
from the next like the princess might have.

suddenly, one by one and all at once, the swans lifted themselves out of the water. they formed a bevy as they sailed upward, preparing to fly over the bridge. i followed this one and that one with my eyes as they traveled in intricate patterns overhead, mighty wings beating chasms into the frigid wind.

one swan flying a bit lower than the rest caught my attention. i only had a few seconds to watch her before every last person on that bridge looked up — startled by the sound of her neck cracking violently against the electric trolleybus wire. she absorbed the impact with wings outstretched and then tumbled belly-first out of the sky. she landed sharply, the softness of her body deadening the thud of her mass against the harsh pavement. blood, thick and sticky like molasses, pooled quickly beneath her as she seized and shivered on the ground.

a lorry approached and the world stopped turning. hundreds of people stood frozen in time, glancing at one another, silently begging someone, anyone, to do something. finally, a young man swooped across the bridge, lifted the dying swan in his arms, and carried her out of the way. the whole world took a breath. paused. and continued on. for them, it was over.

but for me, that swan etched herself into the deepest corners of my mind and bade me never to forget her. i promised her i wouldn't.

and i bought her tiny twin and held her close just to be sure.

peggy

i bought a vintage typewriter that sits
upon my desk, a sixties coronet
someone had painted apple green. with keys
below the fold of my two eager hands,
click-clack and *bing* with every line i scan:
i cannot help but wonder which well-versed,
quick-witted woman's fingers traced letters
before this old machine's new life. i like
imagining that she was called peggy.
she posed with perfect posture as she typed
the memos for the men who ran the place.
but during breaks, her bustling office day
became a tiny sanctuary, where
she wrote a thousand poems, tucked each one
quite carefully away. perhaps afraid
that someone might discover what she hid,
she did the only thing she knew to do.
she quit! and left her stupid, useless job
and vowed to create even more of what
she loved. now i reverse the ribbon — black,
profound, imperfect ink — and hope to write
a few aspiring words with her in mind.

cheyanne leonardo

sunday poem
after laura jean henebry

in an alternate reality i do not ache
and we are spending our sundays
slicing open fresh cantaloupe, heavy
against unsharpened knives
and cutting pieces into tiny cities, placing
dots of blueberry people at the foot
of every skyscraper.
we reach toward each other — eager helianthus — holding,
the way a willow grasps the gleam of full water
sprinkled with sunlight. and, like this,
we walk into the woods, ever as always
unafraid of nightfall; unshuttering
windows we do not have; gathering wildflowers,
ignoring not even the white clover. we fill and
refill the vase, weaving wreaths with what has died.
i sew back the missing buttons, criss-cross stitching
black placket with every color of the sunrise. rip
a hole in the pocket just so i can patch it up with lace.
pull the sleeves away the moment you try
to slide your arms serpentine in.
i start writing the date at the top of my poems because
it no longer hurts to think about the exact day, year —
the passage of time and how we will reconstruct it;
bathe together in the starry amber of remembering.
and you say "i love you" as effortlessly and recklessly
as our river rumbles toward the falls.
without restraint. without
pause.

eclipse

i will behold you as the sky —

though pieces of you are vast
unreachable
unknowable
my gaze is made of tiny telescopes
that trace the ways of suns and stars,
mapping out menageries
of auroras torn asunder (broken
elysian luster) hung
helter-skelter in your heart.

i will learn the contour
of your constellations,
the ellipse of your seasons, search
celestial spheres
for waxing gibbous meaning.

and i will lie down beneath
the far-flung forever,
the elastic shadow of your eclipse
to pray
beyond eternity — in love so
measureless.

pray god i remember this
after mary oliver

and it seems the world over
women are dipping vessels into rivers,
filling them up with something holy.
whether the elixir is drawn from the ganges
or the southern fork of the cumberland;
is carried back to the shrine
or the daisies left at the dogwood's roots: religion
is crafted by the women who wield water,
who siphon it out of mother's veins and
alchemize adhesion.
we whisper words into the air (something between
a spell and a prayer),
commanding creation
to keep you safe. tucked away,
we hold you in the power we conjure. seek out,
stumble upon some kind of magic —
oh, relentlessly real!
written not in runes, rather
sacred similitude.

oracle iv

oh, how the flood rushed in
and woke the wide world
up from a deep sleep — one in which
we did not pray
on two knees for those we love
every day. now,
with a tsunami on my breath
i speak protection into the present,
collect the carnelian
the fluorite
the amethyst
and place the pieces into patterns
that help make sense of the wilderness,
make meaning with all that plagues us.

i am not so special. sometimes
i would rather let the stones speak
and just listen and wait
and write and see
how everything will return to the ocean anyhow.
how each of these rocks i carry around
in a sapphire pouch
will break down. a billion grains of new sand.
crystalline colors
found in fossil hands. and
to think
i was once afraid of the prospect of
undifferentiation. primordial unity.
intoxication.
of losing all this to what i can't envision.
but the smallest mote of me will brave those waves,
offer the armor of a promise such as this:
we will be together in that universe, too.
no matter what crumbs we become, my love —
no water is too wild for me to find you.

backbone

on desperate evenings i have made
an altar of my living room,
knelt in flickering candlelight
and with rainbow palms implored the power
i have once or twice conjured
to protect you.

when i offer your name upward —
quivering wrists rattling totemic beads, secret
syllables between my teeth — i breathe
out
and send the sound to kiss the sky;
watch the wisps of wisdom rise
yet unwritten
only spoken
not from the mouth, rather
deep within the belly of knowing. oh,
there is something.

i cannot differentiate
divine truth from belief.
still, i brandish backbone:
the spine
stem
root
of me.

golden hour

and you sang lucinda
years before words fell
over glowing goldenrod,
before i found myself
in the upside-down of a poem.
looking up at a stitch in the sky
(just an airplane passing by)
but it was something more.
two roads diverged in a yellow wood
and we —
we took both.
drove right over the undergrowth.
through fields full of my favorite color,
the sun dipped into golden hour
and you — always
the master of light — captured
something i believe
only you and i could see.
a spark born between
the friction of your fingertips
and acoustic strings,
sailed by my searching eyes
where i sat watching you sing.
that little flicker-flare came here,
made a home of golden grace
then flew
out of the flowers to greet us,
to meet us face to face. and this time
hidden in the meadow
of sunlit solidago
i heard you ask it to stay.

autumn

i can't run from autumn
though i worship firefly stars
as they turn trees
into songs of summer sky
buds into a body
breaking away from the night
i will have to drink death like water
walk the cold river
honor the rhythm
and listen
as the light wanes
ancient
and sacred
i know forever is a circle
and transition anoints arrival

hero

don't run off alone
and drive desolate highways in search of
some empty house in which to hide

we can only survive together
carry the hero we have in each other
out of the fire and into the night

if you need me, i'll be by the willow tree

if you need me, i'll be by the willow tree,
i say on the sunniest afternoon
we will see for the next few weeks.
it's november now, and i'm still trying
to understand how i got here. holding
on to a kind of gratitude that comes
after mornings spent reaching for you.
and having you reach back,
letting me know a life with you
is finally something i can grasp.

i've been sitting here hoping
the leaves i hear crunching
will turn out to be your footsteps,
making their way toward me.
as if that would be the proof i need:
to watch us take shape beneath this tree.

all i really know
is that it's starting to get cold.
the shadows are shifting,
the light is descending,
and i'm still here alone.
yet i cling unashamedly to the hope
that i will be pulled out of poetic reverie
as you approach. place
your hand on my shoulder and whisper,
we're in this together.
and i would reply simply,
forever.

this is what i want you to understand:
no matter how bad your day was,
i will wait here among the disappearing ducks
until you can bring yourself to show up.
letting me love you means you meet me
when you need someone to talk to,
give me space to make this place with you.

i stretch my toes out toward the willow's roots —
as if writing it down will make it true.

eleven eleven

seven months after i bring you
late spring flowers, bouncing
blue and gold in a wine-bottle vase,
i return to the river. hike
the opposite way
and collect every falling leaf
that lands on this page.

there is a lesson to be learned
from the spot where i sit —
these river rocks that invite me
almost in
to the current,
the rapids
that swallow
the gifts of the trees
and send them
flowing
down the stream.

i take part in the ceremony,
write promises on nature's paper,
intercept their purpose
and release them on their own journey.
this river demands i feed it poetry.
it gives to me and i give back,
ensure our present
won't become the past.

the truth is i don't really know
what i'm doing. i only ever
follow the feeling
until it feels right. (though,
my love, if you were here,
you could capture the light.)

in this moment
i cannot tell the difference
between a vow and a wish.
all i can say is this:
the rhythm of the river
roars even louder,
recalling the day i asked
if you were happy
and you said yes.
please don't forget!
when everything
is falling down around you
and the winds make
dizzy puzzle pieces of your life,
sending them into a raging spin
and flip-flop drop —
i'll always be here on this rock.
that strong and certain bit
that can peek out into the mess,
hold tight until the season rests.

there is nothing i wouldn't give to you
by way of this mystical vein.
you are the reason i am on this earth
at all.
the river reminds
that when we die
there will be somewhere new to fall.

kubrick

i'm still not satisfied by any "answers."
every solution i've ever seen
is just another question
masquerading
as something certain
thanks to simple syntax and
punctuation.

i didn't write the rules.
i'm just trying to write my way
through them
around them
beyond them.
i don't know if my power
reaches any further
than the tip of this pen.

all i can do is keep leaving marks.

consummation

again, the two of us have left the night
and woken up without a single ray
of sun, just candles burning weary light;
these hot and sleepless flames submit to day.
such mornings always come with questions, hushed
and softened. i can see us trying not
to mar enchanted moments, not to rush
away from tightened grips and after-thoughts.
the truth is i am dreaming, though awake,
that one day there will be no after. all
chimera — rosy hope meets deepest ache —
yet humdrum, uninspired, cliché, banal!
this frayed belief consumes my poetry,
but writing forges, forms reality.

the fireplace

we sat legs-crossed before a dying fire.
frail embers burned and took their final breaths
then perished. even swirling smoke grew tired
and ashes asked the heaving haze to rest.
that's when you said my love was somehow flawed,
the ground unsound, just beguiling belief
in something powerful, akin to god —
fantastic or fictitious, illusory

and crudely imagined. yet you recall
the magic now that i sit with my back
to roaring flames, these four prismatic walls,
the scene the same. what must this love have lacked
for you to question my sincerity?
the point is not to answer that. i say
instead: thank god you feel the gravity.
finally! passion sways and stokes the blaze.

love language

i wake up to the sound of you
playing something by beethoven
in the next room. yesterday,
you asked me what i think
about the idea of love languages
and all i really know is that
yours is first and foremost
hands on an instrument,
coaxing loud and unabashed truth
from primordial belly,
cosmic tomb.
but you are fluent in pausing the movie
just to make me a cup of coffee,
holding my hand in a backwoods cemetery,
seeing some kind of beauty in me
when i wish only to hide away.
you take me to perfect places in the forest
and listen to me talk
about the faces i see peeking through rocks.
you pull vocabulary out
of the drawer in your house
where everything is saved:
the poems, the letters,
spinning years of undated days.
grammar takes shape
around a candy cane heart
you haven't moved since june.
around the spills staining
your drawings, phantom flowers,
cowboy boots.
you speak hours-long phone calls
and dinners at midnight,
religious reverence in warm candlelight.
cradling my tired head against your chest,
knowing what wild words are thundering through.
it's never a matter of saying anything. just
simple understanding, darling —
my love language is you.

a star for that

you said, "there is a star for that"
as i sat at your feet
and gazed up at your sublime face —
where god and nature meet.

when you and i traversed these hills,
befriended the night sky,
such far-flung suns were wishing wells
beneath the lunar eye.

my copper coins cast heavenward
as tokens of this love:
an altar made of ether, here
where will wakes fate above.

so lost in possibility
while spheres and shadows shift,
a light that hides reveals one more;
it spins and then it lifts.

now i no longer stretch my neck
to see divinity.
those pennies thrown at distant stars
make a fountain of me.

particles

with you i have traveled
infinite dimensions
between moon and wonder
mercury and heaven
discovered our gravity in constellations
known time through holes
in the cosmic horizon

there are a billion glittering specks
filling our tiny sky
every one a sun
a dream
a body
a year

light shines through the void
and we make our home here

jupiter

jupiter is more passion than planet
crying cold red through the abyss
crafting a song to inspire a symphony of stars

this is not a distant drifting giant
here to fill some space

no — this is a frontier
flying full force
swelling storms
for all the universe to hear

every world is a spirit of sublime scale
another measure of time no telescope can see

violent yet lyrical — a masterpiece
how mass must move in harmony

january

in the early hours of january
i turned the twinkling tunes in your head
into love songs.
"keep it," i said
about the part that leapt, lustrous, into whimsy.
"it's a motif."

i left my old leather journal lying open on your office floor,
my attempt at mapping out a melody — clumsily
etched in ebony —
spilling across the unfurled page.
i was already somewhere dreaming
when you closed the book and placed it on your desk.
eleven years of letters with your name at the crest
sleeping soundlessly
beneath the same sheets as the lyrics we wrote
together.
all my anachronisms
stacked up beside your archives:
a laptop
cassette tapes
emanations.
aeons of psalms waiting for words.

and i yearn to give you something holy.
hallowed and ardent
as the myth i meticulously made
stitching together staccato scraps of our past.
the proof is in the music i let out of my mouth —
where you hear honeyed euphony
emerging as polyphony.

a time for winter
after kait quinn

there is a time for winter,
a time to remember the birth
delivered against a backdrop of death,
like black birds
venturing out as the world reimagines itself in white.

there is a time for winter,
a time to examine the rainbow
arching its spine over the vault of the horizon,
divine and visible,
in view of the trees losing their leaves,
imploring opening eyes to pierce the skyline
and see the other side.

there is a time for winter,
a time to watch the wilting,
welcome the freezing, the shattering,
the cleaving of each season's truths,
learn earth's emerald lesson
and dissolve distinctions between fire and ice.

there is a time for winter,
a time to feel the light lengthen its limber neck,
peek moon by moon
across the rigid hem of darkness,
invite the sun ever-earlier into the unyielding night,
that haunted haven
and revered realm of dreams.

there is a time for winter,
a time to travel
only against the terms of the clock
as it spins, coughing out chronology,
stretching its spectral body over the wayward wheel
and unfolding arbitrary abstractions
in the form of seconds,
spiraling into sundays,
years —

etching an eternity all our own
in the ephemeral glimmer of seraphim snow.

this brief tragedy of flesh
after emily dickinson

not lying in a blackened shroud,
dear death is painted white;
at sunlit fire's mercy not,
but at the whim of ice.

the moment when the branches bend
beneath unwieldy snow,
once-gentle gestures from above
have an oppressive glow.

the weighing down reminds us how
earth gives in great supply,
but there's a line within this life:
to cross it is to die.

we watch the angels as they fall,
expose the weathered bones
laid bare in sacred circles where
our spirits feel at home.

the heaviness of winter says
the body is a sheath.
when this brief tragedy of flesh
weaves breath into a wreath

to hang upon the door of mort
our purpose will be clear.
for now our task is just to learn
how to enjoy it here.

little birds

how can i write you a poem
with no loneliness in it?

i'm here only for the funeral,
for the rhyme of remembering,
the melting
of that lovely frozen wood.

but i too have known this foxglove fire,
the fear that there is more
to put away
than to search for,
that every happy thing held in the heart
must be killed and abandoned —
the calamity
too enormous to carry.
not alone. yet the house is empty.

the days were slow
but the years burst by like little birds
before the poet could stop
and find the words.

a bird or a sailboat

*"i draw a constellation with a piece of chalk,
a bird or a sailboat…"*
-janina diller

it's someone beautiful
baptized by the light perhaps so
that they become the sun
or something close

or it may not be a person at all
rather a creature
with wings that make it magnificent
a bird or a sailboat
a butterfly or even one-hundred of them
florid bodies bathed in sapphire
and ruby and amethyst and jade
emerging from a deep sleep
bursting open then
sailing silently away

it's something awesome and terrible
like ezekiel says a four-faced beast
or flaming rings with fiery eyes
blinking whirling wheeling
and lighting up the skies
yet gentle like dear gabriel
do not be afraid
for he is a myth-maker
a messenger
with messianic words to deliver

it's a guardian who protects you
cushions you in grace
and lifts your car out of the way
but in the same breath
it is a love that ends in death
creating an absence
embodied
ethereal
to go forth and be with god
or at least somewhere away from here
ascended to a great beyond

then maybe even falling
out of deep blueberry sky
like a star
slashing
ashy obsidian night
either condemned in cruel betrayal
or just a glimmer passing by
being wished upon
or waited for
with watchful open hands

caught by the boy at the coffee shop
the woman leading a gospel band
or a pair of princely brothers
from the hills of tennessee

all of what an angel is
adrift in possibility

waiting

you don't know what i do when i'm waiting.
how i kill time with a dull blade

for you are the cynosure. the center.
all that is remaining. persisting.
the breath before every beat.
the origin of gravity.

my weapon — drawn and heavy —
is no match for the absence of light,
the failure to strike,
punch, punish and
slice

open
the same wound, wound
unwavering
around hands that try
to interpret time,
to discern dichotomies between
past and present: living
and dead.

as if our meager measuring
held any meaning
beyond the clicks of the clock —
those little casualties — making graves
of the tiniest increments
with insufficient instruments — oh —

there must be more infinite circles of truth!
perhaps planets,
analog appendages,
turn a temporal key
more ancient than the sun,
the galaxy,
the yearning
for everything
to pull all the world toward
its covetous core,
enhancing always the heart —

the polestar. the marrow.
that myriad, manifold,
untold part.

the softening

i feel myself giving
all the softest parts of me.
sending the tenderness
from my center through my fingertips,
tracing love's armor
along the ballast of your breastbone.

yet i am unable to cushion
or render gentler
the brutal blow,
those slingshot stones
hurled heavy against your heart.

i see the pieces.
the stitches. the reasons.
does love have latitude
in the gaps of grieving?
and what do we lose
in the caesura — the canyon —
the empty spaces cleaving meaning?

in the meantime
my eyes follow the furrows. forlorn,
forgotten —
for you are frozen,
watching
some kind of dizzying disappearing act.
wondering whether the wizard
will find his way back.
not to the beginning.
but to some bright and buoyant place,
simply reminiscent
of antecedent days.

i would reach my hands
beyond the ones that carry our concept of time,
ticking
ever forward
and rip through the elusive scrim
(discord divorced from origin)

because the truth is
you and i are breaking,
aching for the same thing:
that early love unravels
into
the softening.

oracle iii (another anachronism)

an eagle flew overhead moments before
or after the airplane
and again i thought
this is a poem.
one about perspective.
persistence.
permanence.
one in which our communion
did not demand deficient discourse.

even i — whittler
and wielder of words —
can admit their weakness
when it comes to suffusing the soul.
the substance.
the elegiac essence.
still i believe
there is nothing more powerful than poetry.
though i define it differently. broadly.
encompassing all that is holy. which
(if one looks beneath all that we bury)
is everything.

so in lieu of speaking
we spent our time dreaming,
rewriting the rules along the arrows
of our anatomy;
in relation to the roots.
to what is reaching deep
as much as bursting open,
blossoming
out.

anyway i am learning
that reality is an illusion.
and that means if we aren't satisfied
with the surface — the subterfuge
of simplicity —
there are a million more layers to uncover.
and there is space to create another!
one
all our own.
as long as we're willing
to keep digging,

deciding
upon daisies. deathless dandelions.
fermenting forever
within the walls of an emerald city,
a castle of green glass.

though the hour of februus has passed
and purified the pattern,
our sun spins six spheres away from saturn.
tilted
eternally toward
midsummer:
moving
claiming
making
its radiant declaration.
keeping the covenant and
consecrating
continuity.

after all, love
is betrothed to the giver of life,
to the force that delivers us
and uncloaks the clock's wife.

if life is just a dream, let it be this one
after gabrielle m. young

if life is just a dream, let it be this one:
the one where we wake,
enchanted
enraptured
by the seething sunday rain,
braiding and binding the boughs of our bodies,
holding the hierophant
one arm's length away.

i could ask you again about that time last summer
i was walking down your front steps and looked up.
i saw the treetops
aglow with glinting granules,
sublunary stars.
as if our elfin earth had been exalted.
electrified.
i called for you to "come quick!" i said,
"you've got to see this!"
you appeared by my side and found me hypnotized.
"look," i pointed. "magic."
"it's the fireflies," you said.
"they do this every night."
and at first i didn't believe you.
because how could i have gone my whole life
without seeing something so obvious,
so mundane?
how did i have no way to explain
something so simple?

still —
i'd rather believe in the dream.
celebrate the cipher
of this reality.
for i am no fool
stumbling with a white rose
toward my own untimely demise.
(but then again, aren't we all?)

and so we open our eyes.

him not being there

i am crying
cutting the chicken
(in my cubbyhole of a kitchen)
because again i am thinking
about him
not being there.

we are not in the same house anymore
nor am i preparing his meals
but when i feel
the knife
slice
through flesh —

it's as if my own heart is lying
butchered and bloody on the cutting board.
because haven't we both been maimed?
mangled?
one by war, the other —
womanhood.
a wicked world wounded
our raw and wild warmth,
strove to steal our sacred strength.

i am thinking about him not being there
and i miss him
even before he is
gone.
before there is no one

making waffles in the toaster
watching for the mailman
changing the oil checking the tires
falling asleep in the recliner
shooting his shotgun to scare away the strays.

now that i've learned to really see him,
i've been reminded
that one day
i will lose him.

the man who didn't have to be a daddy again.
who chose
the brassy brown-eyed five-year-old
petting the cats on his back porch.
taught her to ride a bike,
built a desk where she could write
and painted the damn thing
bubble-gum pink.
taped on a fringe of white trim.

i am thinking about him not being there —
giving me directions to a place i've been,
warning me about the storm next week — and i
am already
lost, tugged
into
the twister.

i am thinking about him not being there
and i am already grieving.

death beyond a whisper

you see a spirit as she shines
a shroud
a shadow
shimmering
singing like the sun
of some faraway sky

one day on venus
is more infinite
than the heaving howling honey
of the body
the bone
the breath
here to hold the heart
so we can live

give
love
a language
a life
a home

heaven is knowing
death
beyond a whisper

but for now we wonder
and worship the unknown

the crypt

i am mourning
watching this world
move
deeper
into a dimension of darkness
drifting
distant
from incandescent dreams

it is not black like midnight
no — this is the crow's death
a screaming raven
a lonely moon
the blood of the abyss

and i am crying in the crypt
full of dread
that our garden of gravity
will wind up dead
before i can walk

travel

through time
fall into the sun
and melt in the shine

the body of being

i have heard my home called a barren wasteland.
but i look at these trees and see god's hands —

like the time when the twin bradford pears
standing in our front yard
froze over,
split down the middle
and one half of both
fell toward our house at the same moment.
branches crashed against the windows
and my mother woke screaming.

don't tell me the breaking
was anything less than biblical.

together
they were an inseparable pair.
and i had pinned the blooms of both
in my auburn hair
to match the little white flowers
embroidered on my denim dress —
so many sundays!

just one of a billion ways
to talk about god's creation:
the flora and fauna
the force and fervor

the soul of it all.

yet we forget
that our fate
will be to leave one toe in the water.
flesh left to rot and wither
and then
finally
be delivered
into the body of another

being —

become
ourselves
again
and again
and again.

perhaps the mightiest task
is to find the one
we wish to fall with
as we unearth each layer —
digging always deeper
into the mantle of myth.

one mote

here's my advice:
do not let anyone make your world small.

when they come with their buttons,
their rules and regulations,
espousing ludicrous limitations
and try to tighten their ungainly grip
around the neck of what is measureless —

you unclench your fervid fist,
open your hands, stretch fingertips
as far as you can
and tell them this:

"i reach only for the infinite!
the arc that holds all life in it.
and you will not direct my attention
to something one mote lesser than
every last star in the sky.
no. you can go choke
on that fat cat lie."

stanzas and song

since the moment i began
baring my soul to the wide world
and — even bigger than that —
to the town,

i have learned that purpose
is more about the medium
than the message.
like how you and i spend our time
searching — soaking in the depths of rhyme,
distilling all the atoms that we find
into stanzas and song.

i am looking at life as literature,
hearing sighs along the river,
even when i am not sitting
cross-legged in a garden of open books.
belletristic is the breath —
the music —
of breakfast
and gossip
and relationships.

there is semblance
and then there is truth,
which one can carry
in all kinds of containers.

speak again, bright angel

"o, speak again, bright angel, for thou art
as glorious to this night, being o'er my head
as is a wingèd messenger of heaven
unto the white upturnèd wond'ring eyes
of mortals that fall back to gaze on him..."
-romeo, *romeo and juliet* by william shakespeare

you are standing in the kitchen
barefoot on the tile
washing dishes
at the sink, facing me
and the counter becomes a balcony.

the lamplight beams somehow softer,
somehow brighter
(now remember i am a writer)
and it's as if, this time
juliet is the one
with her eyes fixed upon the sun
romancing romeo with tender rhyme.

"speak again, bright angel!" i might remark.
"sing forever as the nightingale
and never as the lark.
give voice to all that only your voice can —
all that the earth of me longs to understand."

and wouldn't i unearth a dagger
in light of the death of your name?
bury the blade in my own heart
and hollow out a grave
where i would surely lay

every word i ever wrote
to broken bloodless rest.
because without you
there is no muse
and nothing to confess.

but in this moment
you are standing in the kitchen
barefoot on the tile
washing dishes.

and i bask in the glow of you
so simply
living.

like unto an emerald

*"and he that sat was to look upon like a jasper
and a sardine stone:
and there was a rainbow round about the throne,
in sight like unto an emerald."*
-revelation 4:3, kjv

a red bird lay bleeding,
dead at your feet
beneath the gleam of green glass

as if the mighty river
froze over — agape and unmoving —
beholding blue bells at the blackest brink
of wilting.

such are the epochs,
the ages of decay.

but i know our love is here to stay
because this was not the first time
that crescent color of life
bloomed before a sanguine song,
against a backdrop awash with blood
in a house they say was built for god.

i have seen it too,
deep in the earth of your eyes —
that sage,
that jade
that rivals the skies!

that was years before i poured the red wine,
soured with fear and indecision — then,
filled the bottle with something
living.

so i can only revel
in the binding and the breaking
knowing we are filling
the hollow with a haven —
now that the venerable vessel
has finally shattered
and all those shards
i always imagined
are not sharp, rather

soft in our hands.
together we sift through them,
erect an emerald altar
and our prayerful prism expands.

the garter snake

who is she?
sitting on her throne
in sea foam robes,
the tide of her dress
stitching a hem
that holds the horn
of lunar luster.

does she even need to pray
with all that light
lying right at her feet?

some say that which appears to the human eye
as the color of the sky
is a reflection of the infinite.

is it really so mysterious?
after all — your shadow is formed
by the absence of illumination:
an empty outline, traced
in your image.

and the happy harmless garter snake
is the serpent guarding the gate,

behind which —
the doors
are wide
open.

enter at your own risk!

though you know what rests behind the veil
because you can conceive of it.

angel falls

at first i pictured an angel
tumbling down a majestic mountainside
spilling into a redeeming river —

not crushed in a heap on the side of the highway.

this was a woman who wrote me a letter,
told me
that the thing connecting all of us
at the soul
heart
root
is a childlike belief in magic.

i could imagine, then —
a waterfall
brightened
by a moonbow,
pulling her in and
sending her
somehow
up —

how that dissevered spirit sprouted wings
and whisked herself gloriously away,

blanketed first by forest
and then
swirling
sparkling
sky.

does every angel learn her name on the same day?

is it so wrong that i could accept the earth
being swallowed by the sun
yet the mere concept of
"nuclear winter"
makes me want to wander
over to the ledge
and just

jump?
the funny thing about the falls is
there isn't one.
just a farcical hiccup in the river.
(they say it used to be a bit bigger
before it was blasted with dynamite
to make way for a canoe race.)

so instead we hoist our bodies onto the boulders
that careless combustion by chance left over

look upon the county's vena cava
and envision ourselves
small like venules
feeling the feral work of a beating heart:

another angel falls
into the belly of art.

dear leann,

thank you for your beautiful letter. i'm sorry
it took me an entire year to write you back.

but now you won't be able to read my reply
because, well, you're dead.

you know, i was thinking about what to write to
you back in early october. the words i hoped
to send your way were finally swirling around
in my mind when, suddenly, it was too late.
those days turned out to be the last few of
your short and precious life. an accident. a
tragedy. you were removed from this world just
as i was learning your name.

if you remember after all this time, you told
me a story in your letter about making friends
at a party in your hometown, where you weren't
really sure if you fit in with the crowd. you
would have no way of knowing this (or maybe you
do) but i began learning the lesson you meant
to teach me in that letter on the very day you
died. call them characters, call them spirits:
either way, the same ones you described were
present with me in the hours after you left
this world. some country boys at a party. i
cradled a grown man's head in my lap when he
felt like he was dying. he came to me for help.
i think because he knew. he saw. there was mag-
ic within and between and all about. and maybe
somehow, together, we moved from seeing it to
finally, really believing it.

speaking of belief, i don't believe in coin-
cidences anymore. i believe in connections. in
tuning in and paying attention. i think you
must have been an expert at that. even though
i never met you, and all i have is that one
letter to remember you by, i wish i could walk
through the woods with you, wander along the
river, and see it all through your eyes. wheth-
er, like daniel, you could read the writing on
the wall, or you were simply noticing that the
shapes you saw scattered about held true mean-
ing -- i think you had something figured out. i
would not be the poet i am without those final
breaths of your wisdom to guide me as i journey
onward. and i will look forward to someday,
somewhere, reaching for your hand.

in this world, there is magic and there is
mystery. somehow, they are inseparable. i will
keep you and your remarkable life in my heart
as i work, letter by letter, to piece it all
together.

ever yours,

cheyanne

acknowledgements

i would like to express my gratitude for a few wonderful
humans who have supported and inspired me throughout my
journey of completing this book.

to rachel clift (@r.cliftpoetry), who once again brought
my vision to life - in a way only a poet could - with her
brilliant design of my manuscript. i could not imagine
entrusting these words to any other soul. thank you for
seeing me, teaching me, and building a beautiful home for
my work.

to laura clift (@l.a.clift), whose writing, art, and cre-
ative spirit never fail to expand my perspective and imag-
ination. thank you for sharing your many ethereal worlds
with me and holding my hand as you walk through mine. i'd
be lost without your courage and insight.

to my dear friends and fellow artistic souls: mellisa
pascale, debbie faires, eric faires, michelle taylor
ayers, josh ayers, jaelyn phillips, andi marie tillman
vestal, jessica rash, whitney swain, and grant swain.
many of you are first readers of my poems, and all of you
are my biggest cheerleaders. thank you all for encourag-
ing me and building me up.

to a few of my fellow poets on instagram: kait quinn
(@kaitquinnpoetry), gabrielle m. young (@g.m.writes), and
laura jean henebry (@betweenthelinesandspaces). thank you
for sharing your work with the world and giving me the
chance to be inspired by your words. the poems in this
collection written after the three of you are some of my
very favorites and highlight this work's most central
themes.

to the amazing crew at gather coffee lounge: kristin,
scott, victoria, ashley, summer, angela, emily, miranda,
boone, rich, nancy, sierra, leondra, ashlynn, and mia.
working with you all has brought me so much happiness and
given me the opportunity to be the best version of myself.
thank you for supporting me and all of our community with
your incredible kindness and hard work.

and to my parents, sharon leonardo and joe goad. thank you
for believing in me, loving me, inspiring me, and giving
me every opportunity to go after my dreams. i love you
very much.

about the poet

cheyanne leonardo is a poet and memoirist located in scott county, tennessee, where she was born and raised. she released her debut poetry collection, more than metaphor, in july 2021, which established her as a small town, appalachian poet with eyes fixed upon investigating the essence of love and life. her work gravitates toward themes of romance, reality, spirituality, memory, travel, identity, language, and the powerful act of writing.

cheyanne holds two master of arts degrees: the first in modern foreign languages and literatures from the university of tennessee, and the second in writing from johns hopkins university. in between her studies, cheyanne lived and worked for two years as an english teacher in stuttgart, germany – an experience that allowed her to travel extensively across europe and gain fluency in german and french. currently, she delights in her job serving coffee and creating meaningful community connections at gather coffee lounge in her hometown.

in addition to her books, cheyanne uses instagram (@cheyannepoetry) to share her work and connect creatively with friends and fellow writers. check out her page to follow along on her journey as a writer, read new poetry, and receive updates on upcoming projects. you can also visit her website at cheyanneleonardo.com for links to her other published works.

pour avancer ce qu'une

bius Virius, lorsqu'il exhorte

poison pour se pa...

lieu de dire que ce pois...

...par une Hésionte p...

délivrera et leur cache

...tatis vino ciboque po...hm...

...pho corpus a cruciatu...

...ndis antiquisque hominibus...

a note on the images

all the images accompanying poems in this text
are photographs taken in and around scott county,
tennessee, by stephen phillips and edited by rachel
clift. most are snapshots of the big south fork
national river and recreation area. can you spot
any familiar places or landmarks?

---

about the designer

rachel clift is a poet, traveler, photographer, &
artist based in the mountains of east tennessee.

she began her journey of writing poetry in 2017 and
has published seven of her own titles and a guided
journal since the summer of 2019. she now freelanc-
es to design books for writers & poets to help them
turn their own manuscripts into works of art.

in the writing world, she is known as r. clift
@r.cliftpoetry & the constellation poet. more than
anything, she longs to inspire people— in some
way, somehow, to love who they are and live life
courageously.

rcliftpoetry.com

write your own poem here
&
share it with me on instagram
@cheyannepoetry